CONTENTS

The Christian Passover

PREFACE

When I tell any truth, it is not for the sake of convincing those who do not know it, but for the sake of defending those that do. ~William Blake

This is my second attempt at writing a book. My first was At Even. At Even was an effort to give a persuasive definition of the biblical use of the term. In over four decades of ministry I have concluded that it is easier to defend the truth than to convince others of it. Truth is always true and never false. Out of this concept is born The Christian Passover, my second attempt. Who knows, what the second time might bring forward. There are a number of misnomers associated with the celebration we Christians call Passover. For me, the quote by William Blake is a perfect fit for what the pages of The Christian Passover deals with. Perhaps you've heard the term Passover Day used, misnomer, there's no such biblical term or day. In this book you're going to read about the Passover in a different light. But most of all you're going encounter some thought provoking truths about what it means to keep a Christian Passover. Brace yourself and be prepared for the introduction of a new paradigm. Perhaps today more than ever Jesus invitation to launch out into the deep is a clarion call to the church. An invitation to abandon traditions born out of that's what our chief prelate taught us approach to biblical truths.   For those of us who grew up celebrating Passover the celebration can become too familiar. It easily slips from a celebration of awe to set of ritualistic practices we perpetuate year after year. Nevertheless the joy and majesty of Passover without controversy can be found in the simplicity of purpose and power in the last supper. So come go with me on a journey through the pages of the Christian Passover and discover. Biblical truths are all around, but do we really see them. We take so much for granted. Launch out into the deep and when you get there maybe you'll be pleasantly surprised. My hope and prayer is that The Christian Passover enlarges your spirit in such a way that it will make a lasting and profound difference in how you understand and celebrate Passover.

"I have chosen the way of truth."
Psalm 119:30 KJV

The Christian Passover

Chapter 1

MY GUIDING STAR

"The art of art, the glory of expression and the sunshine of the light of letters, is simplicity." **Walt Whitman**

We Christians grow up in churches where we take for granted that the teachings of our church. Without question we believe that they are the same as the bible. The bible should be our true guide to truth and not our calcified church teachings. Bible based knowledge is a true liberator and the only way to destroy ancient church paradigms. Over the centuries churches have gotten far away from what is taught in the pages of the bible. Truth as revealed in the bible requires that you open your eyes as to what is not there as well as to what is there. So then we read the pages of the bible concerning Passover and see what we have been told by those who propagate exoteric knowledge. Keep it simple, lift up your eyes and see what's not there. My guiding star for understanding the truths contained in scripture is simplicity. Keeping things simple without sacrificing substance by being overly simplistic, however, can be a challenging undertaking. But if we can reduce the noise and clutter of our own opinions and speculations, the awesome result is a greater understanding with less effort. To often truth is obscured by the fog of theology and a host of religious biases that is so much a part of our Christian experience.

There are some very basic and simple truths about the celebration of Passover that is obscured by the fog of our twentieth century learning experience. I am committed to teaching the Passover in its simplicity, be accurate in my rendering and yet not be naive. Here's a simple truth no where in the bible is there reference to a day called Passover, nor is there any mention of keeping or observing a day called Passover. There is little doubt you can readily call to mind a number of passages in the bible where it mentions keeping the Passover. But what you can't do in fact is read in print, where the bible calls any of those references Passover day. In fact the idea of a Passover day to be kept has its geneses in the biases and preconceived notions you brought with you to the subject at hand and not in what is set before you in print. Keep in mind I haven't said that there isn't a day to be kept as a memorial but rather the day to be observed isn't called Passover. Again I say simplicity is most important in understanding biblical truths. What I try to do is take a very simple evidenced based approach to understanding and teaching Passover. It requires that you not only read and understand what is there but also what isn't. It is hard for religious organizations to say we got it wrong and even harder for churchgoers. When it comes to Passover we got it wrong. However, we can get it right. The Christian Passover is your first step to getting it right. Embracing its simplicity can reveal the truth in scripture. The process of clearing away the excess and clutter of erroneous teachings may seem boring and overwhelming at times. So take a moment to reflect on the need for biblical rightness and truth. This clarity of the need will keep you going when the complexity of getting to simplicity seems too much.

Simplicity is freedom. The bible is a collection of simple truths any complex rendering is of our own devising. When studying the bible the discipline of simplicity results in awareness. It gives us a keen awareness of God's divine purpose and a deeper appreciation of his love toward us. This philosophy, sometimes implicit and sometimes explicit, guides my deliberations and informs the choices that I make on how I live my life. My mother had a saying that "enough is enough and to much stinks". When it comes to understanding scripture too often we're stinking up the place with complexity. No one benefits. Simplicity of life and scripture is truly my guiding star. Why?

"But I fear, lest by any means, as the serpent beguiled Eve through his subtilty, so your minds should be corrupted from the simplicity that is in Christ."
2 Corinthians 11:3 KJV

The Christian Passover

Chapter 2

WORDS MATTER

"All truths are easy to understand once they are discovered; the point is to discover them."
Galileo Galilei

Words matter. Whether written or spoken, regardless of intent, they either bring clarity to or cloud a picture. Allow me to share with you an awkward and embarrassing experience I had in my use of a word. Like many of us whose native language is English, I kind of assumed my vocabulary depth was more then adequate for both spoken and written English. English 101 sometimes called freshman English or college composition. Freshman Year University of Cincinnati one of my early assignments was to write a descriptive essay. Being a master of hastily written essays, in high school, I approached my college assignment with the same vigor. This time my strategy backfired. I decided to paint a word picture of "My Rod Iron Table". I was proud of that rod iron table and wanted everyone to know how beautiful it was. After five hundred words or so of gibberish about, the contour, color and stylishness of "My Rod Iron Table" I said of my paper, "great job". Of course myself adulation dissipated when I received the essay back with about forty redlines through the word rod and underneath each one written the word wrought. The true embarrassment came, however, through the poignant notes at the bottom of the essay. In not so flattering words Professor Katherine Foster let me know that she being one of the few black professors at the university would not tolerate such a careless misuse of words coming from one of the three black students in her class of seventy. She also stopped me at the door and lectured me on why.

How embarrassing! I vowed from that day forward that, before I used a word, any word, I would understand that word and its proper use.

I've shared this personal experience with you not to proclaim a gift of words but rather that understanding: whether of words or any other creature is born from the spirit of discovery. While it is not a very exciting task, word study can be a great way to add new words to your vocabulary and become more familiar with their definitions. A good understanding up front of how a word or phrase is being used is a key to avoiding misunderstandings later.

When the vast majority of any given group, mindlessly adopts the use of a word it strips that word of its true meaning. It wastes the power of the word in its appropriate use. In today's society we live under a constant verbal barrage. It's impossible to ignore the catch phrases of our culture. They enter our minds and speech. In sports, the term is *"great"*. As in, that was a great catch, great pass, or great run. The mindless over use and misuse of a word can spread through a culture like a virus. Over time the word will lose its true meaning. In the Christian Church such a term is *"Passover"*.

In the spirit of sharing, I have discovered that understanding the bible, as is the case with other books requires accurate and rapid retrieval of word meanings (word decoding). Syntax is also an important component of reading comprehension, i.e. how the rules of grammar and word order shape the meaning of a sentence or passage. Another is semantic understanding, it too is a note worthy component of reading comprehension, i.e. understanding the different meanings of individual words. News flash! Words have more than one meaning. A word used in Genesis or in Exodus may or may not have the same meaning in Revelations. The word must be decoded in each individual use to derive the authors intended meaning. E.g. in Genesis the term *evening* (*Hebrew. ereb*) means night or darkness, in Exodus its means the latter part of the day.

It's all Kool-Aid, as a child whenever my friends and I had a powerful thirst we went straight for the Kool-Aid. There was nothing better than a glass of cold delicious Kool-Aid. And there were so many flavors to choose from, grape, orange, cherry, strawberry, lemon-lime; so many flavors. No matter the flavor, however, it was still Kool-Aid. The taste changed with the flavor and the amount of sugar used, but it was all Kool-Aid. Take a word any word and you'll see that it too has many flavors (senses) but its still the same word. Passover is no different, several senses and/or definitions but its still Passover.

When it comes to the power of words to often "we miss the boat", consequently there's lots of miscommunication going on. Words are not to be taken for granted no matter how insignificant they appear to be. Little word clues can point to significant knowledge. Over the years I've come to understand and appreciate the power of words. Our collective understanding of the term Passover has become toxic over the years, thus divesting it of its true meaning and power. I've also come to appreciate the fact that you never learn much until you really want to learn. However, what most of us never come to understand is that knowledge is buried away in words. We fail to recognize that the ability to read comprehensively opens up a new and exciting world. The question Philip asked the eunuch, *"understandest thou what thou readest"*, is the same question each of use must ask ourselves when seeking biblical truths. The eunuch's answer is also apropos *"How can I, except some man should guide me"*. As with my word experience we often need guidance to a clearer understanding. Yes, words matter and the biblical meaning of the word Passover really, really matters. Sadly, too many of us only know what our spiritual leaders have taught us the word Passover mean. Not realizing that we should stop coasting on the training and sermons of our spiritual leaders. This is dangerous to believers and to the Church. All too frequent our personal assumptions color our interpretation of how the bible uses the term Passover. To acquire knowledge we often walk around the thing that is to be studied. I invite you to walk around the word Passover and learn its biblical and true meaning.

"And thus shall ye eat it; with your loins girded, your shoes on your feet, and your staff in your hand; and ye shall eat it in haste: it is the Lord 's Passover." Exodus 12:11 KJV

The Christian Passover

Chapter 3

TRUTH

"Our words are, as a general rule, filled by the people to whom we address them with a meaning which those people derive from their own substance, a meaning widely different from that which we had put into the same words when we uttered them." Marcel Proust

Truth can be altogether elusive and hard to grasp, a wind, a phantom, a mist that disappears into the morning. In order to lay hold on it one must temporarily set aside what they know about a given subject. It is time for a paradigm shift in how we Christians understand and use the term Passover. Let's explore its biblical meanings together.

After years of studying biblical words, Passover in particular, I've settled on some general principles that help me arrive at sound biblical definitions. The first is the unquestioned primacy of context. What is context? Simply put it's the neighborhood in which words hangout. I call it the infrastructure of understanding. It is the words that form the setting of a verse, sentence, or paragraph. Those who fail to understand and appreciate the primacy of context are destined for countless arguments about word-meanings. Immediate context is by far the most important determiner of the biblical definition of a particular word. Whether its written or spoken without proper context the author's intended meaning is often lost. The second principle of importance that I've learned is that meaning is set by the author and discovered by the readers. We are not granted the liberty of determining what someone else meant. This is especially true of the bible. So than in order to derive the authors intent one must interpret the spoken and written word in its literal and plain sense. The third and equally important principle is recognizing the various methods that the bible uses to define words.

There are three basic methods that one can use to arrive at a biblical definition. The bible sometimes defines a word by the direct method, sometimes by comparison and sometimes by contrast. Example of the direct method: "But Sarai was barren; she had no child". (Genesis 11:5 KJV) The word *barren* is defined here, as *"she had no child".* Here's another, however this one involves a phrase but the principle is the same: "And take the helmet of salvation, and the sword of the Spirit, which is the word of God." (Ephesians 6:17 KJV) The definition here of the phrase *"sword of the spirit"* is *"the word of God".* Defining words and phrases directly is a method you'll see used throughout the bible. Here's yet another example: "Then Moses called for all the elders of Israel, and said unto them, Draw out and take you a lamb according to your families, and kill the Passover." (Exodus 12:21 KJV) The word is *"lamb"* the obvious definition here is *"the Passover"*.

Words defined by comparison can also happen at the word, phrase, or clause level. This method is most common in Hebrew poetry and is seen in a style called synonymous parallelism. "Deliver my soul, O Lord, from lying lips, and from a deceitful tongue". (Psalms 120:2 KJV) The word *lying* is defined here by its synonym, *deceitful.* Here's another example of definition by comparison. "And God blessed them, saying, be fruitful, and multiply, and fill the waters in the seas, and let fowl multiply in the earth." (Genesis 1:22 KJV) The word *fruitful* is defined as *multiply*.

Finally let's look briefly at biblical definitions by contrast. "For your obedience is come abroad unto all men. I am glad therefore on your behalf: but yet I would have you wise unto that which is good, and simple concerning evil." (Romans 16:19 KJV) What you see here is *good* and *evil* being contrasted as well as *wise* and *simple*. The obvious meaning here is that a simple person is one who is not wise and an evil person or thing is not good.

The true meaning of Passover, as defined in the Bible, has been corrupted in the common usage of our English. Whether we are consciously aware of it or not, our arguments for our understanding of Passover all follow a certain basic structure. They begin with one or more premises, which are facts that we take for granted. Truth is, we come to different conclusions about this great celebration because we don't use the term *"Passover"* in its biblical sense.

"To the law and to the testimony:
If they speak not according to this word,
It is because there is no light in them."
Isaiah 8:20 KJV

Chapter 4

BIBLICAL DEFINITIONS

"Only wise men look for new wisdom."
Toba Bet

Traditionally, Passover is defined as a seven or eight day spring celebration of the deliverance of Israel out of Egypt, where a special meal is eaten on the holyday. Too often, we over-complicate things in an attempt to display our intelligence, when in reality we end up pushing others away and ultimately losing credibility. We have all heard the phrase, "Keep it simple, stupid." Well it turns out that understanding Passover is not so complicated when we rely on the simplicity of scripture. The bible gives us three definitions for Passover. The first meaning: is the name of the sacrifice

(Lamb), the second meaning of Passover: the killing of the lamb, is called the Lord's Passover and the third meaning: the Feast of Unleavened Bread, is sometimes called the Passover. Through the lens of the aforementioned methods for defining biblical words let's now look at the three biblical usages of the word.

In Exodus twelfth chapter verse eleven we see that Passover is the lamb that is to be killed and eaten. *"And thus shall ye eat it; with your loins girded, your shoes on your feet, and your staff in your hand; and ye shall eat it in haste: it is the Lord 's Passover."* *Again in chapter twelve verse twenty-one we see that the lamb that is to be killed is the Passover.* *"Then Moses called for all the elders of Israel, and said unto them, draw out and take you a lamb according to your families, and kill the Passover."* It is obvious in these two verses that the lamb is called the Passover.

Exodus twelfth chapter verses twenty-six and seven the service of killing the lamb is called the sacrifice of the Lord's Passover. *"And it shall come to pass, when your children shall say unto you, what mean ye by this service? That ye shall say, it is the sacrifice of the Lord 's Passover, who passed over the houses of the children of Israel in Egypt, when he smote the Egyptians, and delivered our houses. And the people bowed the head and worshipped."*

This is also the meaning in Leviticus chapter twenty-three verse five. *"In the fourteenth day of the first month at even is the Lord 's Passover."* It also carries this same meaning in Deuteronomy chapter sixteen verses one and two. *"Observe the month of Abib, and keep the Passover unto the Lord thy God: for in the month of Abib the Lord thy God brought thee forth out of Egypt by night. Thou shalt therefore sacrifice the Passover unto the Lord thy God, of the flock and the herd, in the place which the Lord shall choose to place his name there."* One can readily see the slaughtering of the lamb is called the Lord's Passover.

Ezekiel chapter forty-five verse twenty-one Passover means a seven-day feast in which unleavened bread is to be eaten. *"In the first month, in the fourteenth day of the month, ye shall have the Passover, a feast of seven days; unleavened bread shall be eaten."* Luke chapter twenty-two verse one carries the same meaning. *"Now the feast of unleavened bread drew nigh, which is called the Passover."*

In summary the bible gives three definitions for Passover:

~ The lamb that is to be slaughtered and eaten.

~ The seven days of unleavened bread.

~ The time period in which the lamb is to be slaughtered, called the Lord's Passover.

That's it! These three and only these three definitions of Passover can be found in the bible. They convey the true meaning of Passover and its biblical intent. No holyday to be celebrated or kept called Passover. No Passover day to be found. These concepts and interpretation can only be found in post-biblical uses. There is a definite correlation between the post-biblical use of the word Passover and the controversies that surround its celebration.

"... Today, after so long a time; as it is said, today if ye will hear his voice, harden not your hearts." Hebrews 4:7 KJV

The Christian Passover

Chapter 5

KEEPING PASSOVER

"Bringing to light what had been hidden in darkness should not overwhelm you, but educate you." Solange Nicole

What about keeping Passover? What does it really mean? Many Christians teach that keeping Passover is the observance of a holyday or a weeklong celebration. **However, it does not agree with the bible.** What is the bible's meaning of "keep the Passover" **(in Hebrew literally "do the Passover")**? The answer is a very straightforward and simple one, bring the Passover sacrifice and eat it. Yes, that's correct when Israel was commanded to keep the Passover in Deuteronomy sixteen and one it simply meant bring the sacrifice and eat it. One was said to have kept the Passover when they had eaten of the Paschal Lamb *(in Hebrew the Korban Pesach)*, not just any lamb but the one that was set aside on the tenth day of the first month and specially prepared for the Paschal meal. Though it might seem to be a trivial point it is most important. Why? Because what it means to keep Passover shapes our understanding of the entire celebration. First of all, it eliminates the need for a holy day called Passover. There is no such "animal" the holy day is the first day of the Feast of Unleavened bread. Second of all, it puts the emphasis on the Paschal Lamb, which is exactly what God intended. All other delineations and facets of the celebration draw their identities from the Passover *(sacrificed lamb)*. Third of all, it was so important for each person to eat the lamb *(keep the Passover)* that God gave those who for legitimate causes were not able to keep Passover *(eat the lamb)* another opportunity in the second month. This was not another seven-day celebration but simply another opportunity to eat the lamb *(keep Passover)*. Not withstanding the fact that at one point because of captivity the entire nation of Israel had not kept Passover in the first month. Consequently they celebrated fourteen days of unleavened bread, this celebration was of course and anomaly (see 2Chronicles 30:18).

How did I arrive at these conclusions about what it means to keep Passover? Let's take a closer look. In the twelfth chapter of Exodus verse forty-three thru forty-eight, God gives Moses the ordinance of the Passover, rules governing, keeping the Passover *(eating the Paschal Lamb)*.

"And the Lord said unto Moses and Aaron, This is the ordinance of the Passover: there

shall no stranger eat thereof: But every man's servant that is bought for money, when thou hast circumcised him, then shall he eat thereof. A foreigner and an hired servant shall not eat thereof. In one house shall it be eaten; thou shalt not carry forth ought of the flesh abroad out of the house; neither shall ye break a bone thereof. All the congregation of Israel shall keep it. And when a stranger shall sojourn with thee, and will keep the Passover to the Lord, let all his males be circumcised, and then let him come near and keep it; and he shall be as one that is born in the land: for no uncircumcised person shall eat thereof."

Let's take the time to do a critical analysis of these verses. First thing to notice is that the Lord said to Moses and Aaron that this is the ordinance of the Passover. One can draw from the syntactical structure of verse forty-three that the ordinance is about the lamb and who can eat it. No stranger can eat the lamb. So it is easily surmised that the ordinance is not concerned with the celebration of a day nor is it focused on a weeklong celebration. Verses forty-four and forty-five are more of the same. Verse forty-six turns to where to eat the lamb, in the house only, without breaking any of its bones. Verse forty-seven the term *"keep it"* is introduced. What are they keeping? Obviously, the command to eat the lamb in accordance with the rules set forth by ordinance. Verse forty-eight tells us that in fact what they are doing, including the stranger that is in compliance with the ordinance, is keeping the Passover unto the Lord. So we can safely conclude to *"Keep Passover"*, meant to bring the sacrifice and eat it.

Flawed or incomplete information leads to flawed conclusions. When it comes to Passover this fact has never been so vividly important. Paradigms die hard especially flawed ones. Try as we may many of us find it hard to rid ourselves of our biases and habits of mind. Let's look into the "looking glass" of biblical facts one more time. This time let's analyze Numbers ninth chapter verses six thru fourteen.

"But there were certain men, who were unclean by the dead body of a man, so that they could not keep the Passover on that day; and they came before Moses and before Aaron on that day. And those men said unto him: 'we are unclean by the dead body of a man; wherefore are we to be kept back, so as not to bring the offering of the LORD in its appointed season among the children of Israel?' And Moses said unto them:' stay ye, that I may hear what the LORD will command concerning you.' And the LORD spoke unto Moses, saying: 'Speak unto the children of Israel, saying: if any man of you or of your generations shall be unclean by reason of a dead body, or be in a journey afar

off, yet he shall keep the Passover unto the LORD; in the second month on the fourteenth day at dusk they shall keep it; they shall eat it with unleavened bread and bitter herbs; they shall leave none of it unto the morning, nor break a bone thereof; according to all the statute of the Passover they shall keep it. But the man that is clean, and is not on a journey, and forbeareth to keep the Passover, that soul shall be cut off from his people; because he brought not the offering of the LORD in its appointed season, that man shall bear his sin. And if a stranger shall sojourn among you, and will keep the Passover unto the LORD: according to the statute of the Passover, and according to the ordinance thereof, so shall he do; ye shall have one statute, both for the stranger, and for him that is born in the land."

In Verse six the men are troubled by the fact that they are unclean and are prohibited by the Passover ordinance from keeping

Passover. In verse seven the men make it clear what their main concern is, the fact that they cannot bring the Passover sacrifice. Notice the focus is not on the celebration of the day but the sacrifice. The day draws its significance from the fact that it is the day the sacrifice is to be brought and eaten. In verse eight Moses says let me check with the Lord. In verses nine, ten and eleven the Lord gives him his answer, saying they should keep the Passover in the second month. Notice how the phrases *keep it* and *eat it* are used synonymously, the "*it*" is of course the Passover.   Let's restructure the eleventh verse, by inserting the proper noun *Passover* for its pronoun *it*. With a minor adjustment verse eleven would read as follows:

The fourteenth day of the second month at even they shall keep Passover, and eat Passover with unleavened bread and bitter herbs.

Once again we see that keeping the Passover and eating the Passover are one in the same. Verses twelve thru fourteen are more of the same, who is eligible to eat Passover and who is forbidden by ordinance. Feeling confused, are you? Just a bit more clarity, you say. Well let's look in the New Testament to see if we see the same structure and usage.

Matthew chapter twenty-six verses eighteen thru twenty-one might bring a bit more clarity to the subject. Let's see.

"And he said, Go into the city to such a man, and say unto him, The Master saith, my time is at hand; I will keep the Passover at thy house with my disciples. And the disciples did as Jesus had appointed them; and they made ready the Passover. Now when the even was come, he sat down with the twelve. And as

*they did eat, he said, Verily I say unto you,
that one of you shall betray me."*

Verse eighteen the Passover is being kept in
the house and is being prepared and eaten.
Notice, keeping Passover is not a
celebration but the act of preparing and
eating the Paschal lamb. Matthew, Mark,
Luke and John all refer to the Passover as
what is to be eaten, not in respect of a day
to be celebrated. Of course there is a day to
be memorialized, however the fact is the
bible doesn't call it Passover. The concept
of a day called Passover is an extra-biblical
one, consequently every time we read or
hear the term *keep Passover* we conjure up
the notion of a day to be celebrated. When
in fact to keep Passover, in its biblical
context, simply meant to kill the lamb and
eat it.

"And he sent Peter and John, saying, Go and prepare us the Passover, *that we may eat."*
Luke 22:8 KJV

The Christian Passover

Chapter 6

LEST WE FORGET

"Far-called, our navies melt away; on dune and headland sinks the fire: Lo, all our pomp of yesterday is one with Nineveh and Tyre! Judge of the Nations, spare us yet, lest we forget—lest we forget!" Rudyard Kipling

Memorials commemorate great people and great events in history. Short on memory we tend to forget what God has done for us, for this reason God instituted memorials, *"lest we forget"*. There are three commemorative components of the Feast of Unleavened bread, which is called the Passover, (see Luke 22:1).

They are:

~The eating of the lamb on the night the death angel passed over the homes that had the Paschal Lamb's blood on their doorpost.

~The commemorative holyday marking the day that Israel went into and came out of Egypt four hundred and thirty years later.

~The seven days of eating unleavened bread, reminding Israel of the haste in which they left Egypt.

When studying the Passover, there are some important points or "**keys**" to keep in mind. Neglect of these points has lead to much confusion.

Key Number One ~ The night of the death angel was to be memorialized with a commemorative supper.

"It is a night to be much observed unto the Lord for bringing them out from the land of Egypt: this is that night of the Lord to be observed of all the children of Israel in their generations." Exodus 12:42 KJV

"And they shall eat the flesh in that night, roast with fire, and unleavened bread; and with bitter herbs they shall eat it. Eat not of it raw, nor sodden at all with water, but roast with fire; his head with his legs, and with the purtenance thereof. And ye shall let nothing of it remain until the morning; and that which remaineth of it until the morning ye shall burn with fire." Exodus 12:8 – 10 KJV

Key Number Two ~ The day Israel came out of Egypt was to be memorialized with a holy convocation and no leavened bread was to be eaten.

"And this day shall be unto you for a memorial; and ye shall keep it a feast to the

Lord throughout your generations; ye shall keep it a feast by an ordinance forever. Seven days shall ye eat unleavened bread; even the first day ye shall put away leaven out of your houses: for whosoever eateth leavened bread from the first day until the seventh day, that soul shall be cut off from Israel. And in the first day there shall be an holy convocation, and in the seventh day there shall be an holy convocation to you; no manner of work shall be done in them, save that which every man must eat, that only may be done of you. And ye shall observe the feast of unleavened bread; for in this selfsame day have I brought your armies out of the land of Egypt: therefore shall ye observe this day in your generations by an ordinance forever. In the first month, on the fourteenth day of the month at even, ye shall eat unleavened bread, until the one and twentieth day of the month at even." Exodus 12:14 – 18 KJV

"And Moses said unto the people, Remember this day, in which ye came out from Egypt, out of the house of bondage; for by strength of hand the Lord brought you out from this place: there shall no leavened bread be eaten. This day came ye out in the month Abib."
Exodus 13:3 – 4 KJV

Key Number Three ~The unleavened bread was to memorialize the fact that Israel left Egypt in haste.

"Thou shalt eat no leavened bread with it; seven days shalt thou eat unleavened bread therewith, even the bread of affliction; for thou camest forth out of the land of Egypt in haste: that thou mayest remember the day when thou camest forth out of the land of Egypt all the days of thy life." *Deuteronomy 16:3 KJV*

Key Number Four ~ The Passover was to be killed on the first day of the feast of unleavened bread, at the going down of the sun.

"And there shall be no leavened bread seen with thee in all thy coast seven days; neither shall there any thing of the flesh, which thou sacrificedst the first day at even, remain all night until the morning." Deuteronomy 16:4 KJV

"And the first day of unleavened bread, when they killed the Passover, his disciples said unto him, Where wilt thou that we go and prepare that thou mayest eat the Passover?" Mark 14:21 KJV

"But at the place which the Lord thy God shall choose to place his name in, there thou shalt sacrifice the Passover at even, at the going down of the sun, at the season that thou camest forth out of Egypt." Deuteronomy 16:5 KJV

Key Number Five ~ Sabbaths are to be celebrated from even unto even, in other words from sunset to sunset or from twilight to twilight.

"Also on the tenth day of this seventh month there shall be a day of atonement: it shall be an holy convocation unto you; and ye shall afflict your souls, and offer an offering made by fire unto the Lord." Leviticus 23:27 KJV

"It shall be unto you a Sabbath of rest, and ye shall afflict your souls: in the ninth day of the month at even, from even unto even, shall ye celebrate your Sabbath." Leviticus 23:32 KJV

This is the same construct that is used for all the holydays; the celebration begins at the going down of the sun on the day prior to the actual holyday.

"In the first month, on the fourteenth day of the month at even, ye shall eat unleavened

bread, until the one and twentieth day of the month at even." Exodus 12:18 KJV

"In the fourteenth day of the first month at even is the Lord 's Passover. And on the fifteenth day of the same month is the feast of unleavened bread unto the Lord: seven days ye must eat unleavened bread." Leviticus 23:5-6 KJV

Key Number Six – The entire celebration is for seven days whether it is referred to as Passover or Feast of Unleavened Bread; it is still only seven days.

"In the first month, in the fourteenth day of the month, ye shall have the Passover, a feast of seven days; unleavened bread shall be eaten." Ezekiel 45:21 KJV

"And the children of Israel that were present at Jerusalem kept the feast of unleavened

bread seven days with great gladness."
2Chronicles 30:21 KJV

Any approach to the study of Passover that ignores these six key points is flawed in its inception and will no doubt result in a flawed understanding of this great freedom celebration.

"Thus saith the Lord, Stand ye in the ways, and see, and ask for the old paths, where is the good way, and walk therein, and ye shall find rest for your souls. But they said, we will not walk therein." Jeremiah 6:16 KJV

Chapter 7

HONOR THE SACRIFICE

"Once a year we honor the sacrifice, else we forget the God of our salvation. An odyssey of faith, a spiritual journey that takes us from the Paschal Lamb to the Lamb of God."
Larry C. Hamner

Over the years I have come to value the typological picture of the paschal lamb as being one of the most vivid depictions of God's love for his people. This is evident in the way the Holy Spirit develops the narrative of the sacrificial lamb and the Lamb of God throughout the scriptures. The storyline of scripture is that God has always had a prepared lamb, ready and willing to make the ultimate sacrifice, for his people. We see the inadequacy of the blood of the paschal lamb that it could not take away our sins. But we also see the power of the cross, the offering of the body of Jesus Christ once and for all to sanctify us unto eternal salvation. It is the odyssey of the lamb that helps us to better understand the blessing of the New Covenant.

Should Christians keep Passover? Lately there has been an inordinate amount of interest by mainstream Christianity in the biblical festivals. Turn on your radio or television come festival time you'll hear and see the new found interest in their programming.   Although I have no inside privilege to this explosion of interest in the biblical festivals, I believe much of it is due to the abundance of information at our fingertips. Before we had computers in our pockets, we had to find things out the hard way. In the not so distant past truth was discovered by immersing oneself in the quest for it, consequently there were few who made the sacrifice. Because of this dearth of ready information mainstream Christianity cleaved to its pagan based holydays. However, a growing number of Christians are rejecting the historical arguments as to why they shouldn't celebrate the biblical festivals.   For this reason the Christian Church now has a monumental need for a radical revision of some of her inherited teachings. At the head of the parade toward change is the Passover. Much of the objection to a Christian Passover is derived from the idea that it is a Jewish celebration and not a Christian celebration. This is another one of those hard to kill paradigms. The scripture is very clear on this question.

"Speak unto the children of Israel, and say unto them, concerning the feasts of the Lord, which ye shall proclaim to be holy convocations, even these are my feasts"
Leviticus 23:2 KJV

Both Jews and Christians need to recognize the fact that these are God's celebrations and no one group has ownership. One should also understand that all other celebrations are traditions of man and should not be celebrated in lieu of God's holy festivals. Here in lies the majesty and beauty of prophecy and scripture. Consider Daniel's vision and prophecy concerning this very subject.

"And he shall speak words against the Most High, and shall wear out the saints of the Most High; and he shall think to change the seasons and the law; and they shall be given into his hand until a time and times and half a time." Daniel 7:25 JPS

Now look at God's instruction concerning The Passover.

"Thou shalt therefore keep this ordinance in its season from year to year." Exodus 13:10 JPS
"'Let the children of Israel keep the Passover in its appointed season." Numbers 9:2 JPS

With the advent of gentiles in the Church, came also the influence of the traditions they brought with them. Exacerbated by pressure from the politicians of the day the idea that Jews were "Christ Killers" became entrenched in Christian "church-lore". Thus the Church began to reject any and everything Jewish. Additionally, virtually all Christian Churches began to promote the idea that Christianity had replaced Judaism, therefore, abrogating the need to observe the law and its festivals. Consequently, Christianity drifted into what we have today, the traditions of man. Well-said Daniel, they *"thought to change seasons and the law".* Could it be that we have a renaissance on the horizon with the

warming of the Christian Churches to the
biblical festivals?

Could it be the end of Daniel's *"time and
times and half a time"?* If Christians are
truly awakening from a spiritual slumber
and opening their eyes to the splendor and
majesty of God's holy festivals then there is
a great need for understanding of the
Christian Passover and what it truly means
to keep it.

Early on I wrote about the slipperiness of
word meanings and how it has affected our
use of the term Passover and territorialized
our understanding of the celebration. I was
specifically focused on Israel and the
celebration that God commanded them and
what it meant to keep Passover through the
eyes of an ancient Israelite. I concluded that
for an ancient Israelite to keep Passover
simply meant to kill and eat the Paschal
Lamb on the first night of The Feast of

Unleavened Bread. It is my belief that in order to understand the present we must first understand the past. God forbid that I should leave you thinking that in order to keep Passover Christians must kill a lamb and eat it. It is imperative that we now look at "The Christian Passover" post crucifixion. In so doing perhaps we will uncover a new paradigm for a Christian Passover. Maybe just maybe we will see an outstretched arm that reaches from generation to generation. Maybe just maybe we will remember the cross. Maybe just maybe all of Christendom will stop to remember the sacrifice in its season.

"And looking upon Jesus as he walked, he saith, Behold the Lamb of God." John 1:36 KJV

The Christian Passover

Chapter 8

BEHOLD THE LAMB OF GOD

"The idea of redemption is always good news, even if it means sacrifice or some difficult times. " Patti Smith

Passover is truly all about honor and remembrance. On Passover we honor the sacrifice, the death of one for the freedom and salvation of many, the perfect for the imperfect. With a brutal death on the cross-looming Jesus had a burning desire to eat Passover with his disciples. He wanted to participate in this final tribute to the Paschal Lamb.

"And he said unto them, With desire I have desired to eat this Passover with you before I suffer: For I say unto you, I will not any more

eat thereof, until it be fulfilled in the kingdom of God. And he took the cup, and gave thanks, and said, Take this, and divide it among yourselves: For I say unto you, I will not drink of the fruit of the vine, until the kingdom of God shall come." Luke 22:15 – 18 KJV

It is important for us as followers of Jesus to never forget his "Last Supper Request."

"And he took bread, and gave thanks, and brake it, and gave unto them, saying, this is my body which is given for you: this do in remembrance of me. Likewise also the cup after supper, saying, this cup is the new testament in my blood, which is shed for you." (Luke 22:19-20 KJV)

When Jesus made this request it was undoubtedly first to the disciples and, in turn to all future believers. Thus establishing his death on the cross as the redemption story that he wanted his disciples to remember. Let me digress here for a moment to highlight the transition that is taking place at this last supper. Take another look at Luke chapter twenty-two verses fifteen thru eighteen and perhaps you'll see what I see. A noteworthy shift of focus is taking place. Jesus takes the Passover focus off the Paschal Lamb of Egypt. He then in verses nineteen and twenty turn it to the Lamb of God. In other words he took away the first to establish the second, the Paschal Lamb for the Lamb of God. Paul no doubt understood the change. He writes.

"Purge out therefore the old leaven, that ye may be a new lump, as ye are unleavened. For even Christ our Passover is sacrificed for us." 1Corithians 5:7 KJV

Seeing that Christ is our Passover and if Christians are to keep Passover.   Then it follows that if for ancient Israel to keep Passover simply meant to kill the Lamb and eat it, so it is with the Christian Passover. However, we Christians are blessed in that we don't have to kill the lamb anymore.

"And all that dwell upon the earth shall worship him, whose names are not written in the book of life of the Lamb slain from the foundation of the world." Revelations 13:8 KJV

Our lamb has already been slain for the supper we have only to eat his flesh and drink his blood. And how do we eat Christ? He that has an ear let him what the spirit is saying to the church.

"I am the living bread which came down from heaven: if any man eat of this bread, he shall live for ever: and the bread that I will give is my flesh, which I will give for the life of the world." John 6:51 KJV

"Then Jesus said unto them, Verily, verily, I say unto you, except ye eat the flesh of the Son of man, and drink his blood, ye have no life in you. Whoso eateth my flesh, and drinketh my blood, hath eternal life; and I will raise him up at the last day. For my flesh is meat indeed, and my blood is drink indeed. He that eateth my flesh, and drinketh my blood, dwelleth in me, and I in him." John 6:53 – 56 KJV

"And when he had given thanks, he brake it, and said, take, eat: this is my body, which is broken for you: this do in remembrance of me." 1Corinthians 11:24 KJV

Eating the "flesh" and drinking the "blood" of Jesus is how Christians Keep Passover. The hyperbole that Jesus used of eating his flesh and drinking his blood symbolizes the new and greater Exodus that was gained at the expense of his shed blood and broken body. The gospel of Luke identifies this

"New Covenant Passover" as the broken bread and cup after supper, Paul in First Corinthians chapter eleven verse twenty calls it the "The Lord's Supper". In saying, "this is my body which is given for you: this do in remembrance of me" Jesus is saying the Passover is now about him and the great salvation that God is going to provide through his sacrifice. In the first Passover it was the sacrifice of a lamb without blemish in order that the first-born of Israel might live.

In this final Passover event God gives his only son that we might live, he too being a lamb without blemish. But his death was not only about paying for our sin; it was also about establishing the New Testament Church. The Lord's Supper shows the conception of the New Testament Church, while Pentecost announces its birth. As the first Passover memorialized God calling out a people to him, so the Christian Passover memorializes Jesus calling out a people unto him. He has called us to a total and complete freedom not to the Jew only but to as many that will believe. To as many as will set at the Lord's Table and partake of his freedom supper there's a promise of life. A world without end!

"The next day John seeth Jesus coming unto him, and saith, Behold the Lamb of God, which taketh away the sin of the world"
John 1:29 KJV

Chapter 9

CHRIST OUR PASSOVER

"Though no one can go back and make a brand new start, anyone can start from now and make a brand new ending."
Attributed to Carl Bard

My goal for writing this book was to bring distinctness and clarity to how the bible uses the term Passover. I wanted to also point out the subtleness of word meanings, same word but slightly different meanings, dependent on the syntactical and semantic context. Words change meaning overtime and Passover is one of those words. In bible times the word Passover meant the sacrifice, the time the sacrifice was to be killed and the seven-days of the feast of unleavened bread. In this post-biblical age it has somehow come to mean a holyday celebrating the exodus of Israel from Egypt as well as the seven-days of unleavened bread. I've also tried to show that to biblical Israel *" keep Passover"* or literally *"to perform or do Passover"* meant to kill the Paschal Lamb and eat it. Thus the same meaning is carried over into the Christian Passover. Seeing that Christ our Passover was sacrificed for us, in order to *"keep Passover"* Christians must eat Christ. How does one do that? Eat Christ that is. Jesus supplied the answer for us *"And when he had given thanks, he brake it, and said, take, eat: this is my body, which is broken for you: this do in remembrance of me"*. It is through the Lord's Supper that we eat Christ, thus keeping the Christian Passover. This precious and life-creating sacrament stands forever as a memorial to Jesus Christ the Majestic Lamb of God. It follows then that we should keep it in its season, once a year, during the first night of the feast of unleavened bread.

If you can see and understand the simple truths about Passover outlined in this book, you'll come to a greater appreciation for Passover and its significance to the Christian Church. God has given the life of his son as a special gift to The Church and we should never forget the sacrifice. Jesus our *"Passover"* asked that we remember Calvary through the service we call communion which is *"the broken bread and blessed cup".* We end with the words of Paul the Apostle as he urges the New Testament Church to keep Passover.

"Therefore let us keep the feast, not with old leaven, neither with the leaven of malice and wickedness; but with the unleavened bread of sincerity and truth." 1 Corinthians 5:8 KJV

www.ingramcontent.com/pod-product-compliance
Lightning Source LLC
Chambersburg PA
CBHW071429040426
42445CB00012BA/1313